Tonita Peña

Tonita Peña, c. 1935. Photography by T. Harmon Parkhurst. Museum of New Mexico Fine Arts Collection, negative #46988.

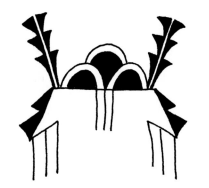

Tonita Peña

Quah Ah

1893 - 1949

by Samuel L. Gray

Avanyu Publishing Inc.

Cover: Harvest Dance, undated. Watercolor. 13 x 20 inches.
Adobe Gallery. Photography by Focus Studio.

Copyright 1990   **AVANYU PUBLISHING, Inc.**
P.O. Box 27134
Albuquerque, New Mexico 87125
(505) 243-8485   (505) 266-6128

Printed in the United States of America.   First Edition
First Printing 1990

Library of Congress Cataloging in Publication Data

Tonita Peña / [edited by] Samuel L. Gray.
           p.   cm.
           Includes bibliographical references.
           ISBN 0-936755-08-3 : (hardback) $39.95
           ISBN 0-936755-17-2 : (paperback) $29.95
1. Peña, Maria Antonia, 1893-1949. 2. Artists, Pueblo—New
Mexico—Cochiti Pueblo—Biography. 3. Pueblo Indians—Art.
4. Pueblo Indians—Biography. 5. Cochiti Pueblo (N.M.)—Biography.
I. Gray, Samuel L., 1911-
E99.P9P397 1989
759.13—dc20
[B]   89-48719
                                                                           CIP

iv

To Grace

Untitled (Harvest Dancer), c. 1935. Watercolor. 8 x 6 inches. The Heard Museum Collection IAC #35.

Table of Contents

List of Illustrations   ix

Foreword   xi

Preface   xiii

Acknowledgments   xv

1. INTRODUCTION   1

2. A PUEBLO ARTIST   7

3. PERSONAL RECOLLECTIONS of Howard and Mike Shaw   29

4. PERSONAL RECOLLECTIONS of Pablita Velarde   51

5. PERSONAL RECOLLECTIONS of Her Children   59

6. SIGNATURES   65

7. HER ART   67

Appendix A—Selected Exhibitions   73

Appendix B—Selected Collections   75

References   77

Genealogy   Back Endsheet

Basket Dance, c. 1919. Watercolor. 11 1/2 x 15 inches. James T. Bialac Collection.
Photography by Jerry Jacka.

List of Illustrations

Tonita Peña, c.1935.   ii
Untitled (Harvest Dancer), c.1935.   vi
Basket Dance, c. 1919.   viii
Lightning Dance (identified as Gourd Dance), c.1920.   2
Making Pottery, c.1918.   3
Eagle Dance, undated.   4
Buffalo Dance, c.1935.   5
Buffalo Dance, undated.   6
Pair of matched large pots.   9
Hopi Dance (Tomahawk), undated.   11
Map of Rio Grande Pueblos.   13
Black on red jar by Tonita, c.1910.   14
Eagle Dance—Cochiti, c.1932.   17
Children of Tonita Peña, Cochiti Pueblo, c.1934.   18
Family of Tonita Peña, Cochiti Pueblo, c.1934.   19
Corn Dancer—Male, c.1933.   22
Corn Dancer—Female, c.1933.   23
Peter Rabbit drawings.   24
Peter Rabbit drawings.   25

Tonita paints on canvas. Untitled, c.1935.   26
Eagle Dancer, c. 1935.   26
Cochiti Pueblo Eagle Dancer, c.1941.   27
Koshare, c.1930.   28
Harvest Dance, undated.   31
Bow and Arrow Ceremony, Cochiti, undated.   32
Deer Mother Dancer, undated.   33
Deer Dance, c.1925-30.   35
Untitled, undated.   36
Untitled (Buffalo Dance), undated.   37
Paintings of Cochiti pottery, c.1940.   41
Basket Dance, undated.   43
Buffalo Dance, c.1926.   44
Pottery bowl made by Tonita.   46
Untitled, c.1940.   47
Epitacio Arquero, Joe Herrera Jr., Tonita Peña and Howard Shaw.   49
Navajo Dance, 1920.   53
San Ildefonso Comanche Dance, c.1942.   54
Cochiti Pueblo Eagle Dance, undated.   55
Cochiti Pueblo Dancers, c.1920s.   56
Straight Dance, 1919.   58
Tonita at work, c.1942.   60
Making Tissue Bread, 1918.   62
Tonita at home.   64
Animal Dance, c.1925.   68
Untitled (Cochiti Pueblo Indian Plaza Dance), undated.   69
Victory, c.1943.   70
Missionary Greeting Pueblo Indians, c.1940.   71

Foreword

For as long as I have known Sam Gray his excitement and enthusiasm for Southwest Indian peoples, their culture, and history were much in evidence. Though he studied anthropological and historical writings in depth, more important were his firsthand experiences throughout the Southwest which acquainted him with the descendants of the region's original inhabitants. Growing up in New Mexico, he was drawn to the people of the Rio Grande and among these he especially came to admire and respect the work and life of Tonita Peña.

Tonita Peña is considered by many to be the first woman painter among the Rio Grande Pueblo people, one whose work is extremely well regarded from the time she began painting, shortly after 1916, to her death in 1949. Yet no book has been written which focuses directly upon her life and accomplishments as an artist. Too often, Tonita Peña appears as a brief note in the history of Pueblo painting.

With this volume, Sam Gray begins to remedy this omission by bringing together unpublished archival materials, written and recorded reminiscences of individuals close to her, as well as his insights developed from his longstanding fascination with the Pueblo Southwest. He presents his personal perspective of Tonita Peña the artist and member of Cochiti and San Ildefonso pueblos. Not only does the volume serve to introduce Tonita Peña to a public increasingly interested in the evolution of southwestern painting through one of the founders of the easel art tradition, but it also provides intriguing glimpses into her life as a vital member of the pueblo community to which she belonged. A more complete picture of the woman behind the artist emerges in which the forces shaping her art, whether community dances or scenes depicting daily domestic tasks, found their most eloquent expression on paper as watercolors.

Sam Gray, in telling the story of Tonita Peña, acquaints us with an amazing Pueblo woman who, early in the twentieth century, established herself as an artist of note, a pioneer who would influence generations of painters to follow.

Anne I. Woosley, Ph.D.
Director, The Amerind Foundation

Preface

It seems that every book we publish introduces us to new avenues in the publishing business. With this one, our tenth book, we experimented with *desktop publishing*, designing and laying out the manuscript and artwork on our computer. We have come a long way!

We are particularly pleased to publish *Tonita Peña* for several reasons.

As the first female Pueblo Indian painter, Tonita is long overdue for recognition with a book on her life and her art. She made monumental contributions toward gaining appreciation of early easel art of New Mexico's Pueblo Indian artists. She was among the very first of the Southwest Indians who established a unique style of painting which is now so intimately associated with New Mexico Pueblo Indians. It is our wish that recognition be given to the other early artists who were Tonita's contemporaries.

Secondly, it gives us pleasure to publish Sam Gray's first book. Having known Sam for over 15 years, sharing in his memories of early New Mexico history and his enthusiasm for Pueblo Indian art, it is now our pleasure to share this new milestone in Sam's life. We congratulate him on undertaking such a monumental task.

Thirdly, we are happy to add a new subject to our list of books. To date, our titles have included subjects of history, Navajo weaving, reservation traders, ceremonial functions and objects, and prehistoric pottery.

We hope *Tonita Peña* will give new insight to artists, collectors, and dealers on the background and inspiration of early New Mexico Pueblo artists.

Alexander E. Anthony, Jr.   J. Brent Ricks

Acknowledgments

I wish to express my sincere appreciation to the following persons and institutions for their cooperation, without whose assistance and encouragement this book would not have been possible.

It would have been difficult indeed to complete this book without the collaboration of Tonita's son, Joe H. Herrera. Not only did he furnish much personal information concerning his mother, he also provided cherished photographs of Tonita and identified dances depicted in his mother's paintings.

I also wish to thank Tonita's daughter, Victoria Melchor, for her permission to use her beautiful letter to me reliving her early life with her mother and father at Cochiti.

In addition, credit should be given to Tonita's other children and grandchildren for aiding in the compilation of her genealogy chart included as an endsheet of this book.

Thanks also to:

The late Lt. Col. Howard Shaw and his wife, Ida Mae Shaw, of Santa Fe, for help in preparing the chapter on their relationship with Tonita.

John and Vivian Ross of Albuquerque who saved me from starvation and sleeping in the streets while on many of my research trips.

Keith and Carol Hill of Albuquerque for joining me on many research trips to Cochiti and Santa Fe and for their inspiration in my writing.

George and Peg Koppmann of Santa Fe, for their generosity in giving me a home to use while in Santa Fe.

The Catholic priests of the parish church in Peña Blanca, west of Cochiti Pueblo, for permitting me to research their parish records.

The Church of Jesus Christ of Latter-Day Saints for furnishing me with access to films of the Catholic Church records for San Ildefonso and Cochiti at their Genealogical Library in Albuquerque and in Tucson.

Elizabeth Caryl of Green Valley, Arizona, for her patience and fortitude in transcribing the most difficult of my research tape recordings.

Lynn T. Brittner, Collections Manager, Indian Arts Research Center, School of American Research, Santa Fe, for notes of Dr. Kenneth Chapman pertaining to Tonita Peña, Martina Vigil, and Maria Martinez, and for slides of Tonita Peña's paintings.

James T. Bialac of Scottsdale, Arizona, for his generosity and support in allowing me to use and study his paintings by Tonita Peña, and for his valued critique and advice in the preparation of this text.

Dr. Anne Woosley, Director, The Amerind Foundation, Dragoon, Arizona, and her husband, Allan McIntyre, Collections Manager, for access to the Foundation's library, slides of Tonita Peña's paintings and for their enthusiastic encouragement when my problems seemed insurmountable.

Ann E. Marshall, Curator of Collections, The Heard Museum, Phoenix, Arizona, for access to slides of Tonita Peña's paintings.

Elizabeth C. Hadas, Director, University of New Mexico Press, Albuquerque, for reviewing the manuscript and for her constructive criticism thereof.

Sandra D'Emilio, Curator, New Mexico Museum of Fine Arts, Santa Fe, for searching and finding pictures of Tonita Peña's paintings and for securing slides for my use.

Heather F. Anthony of Albuquerque, for editing and typing the manuscript and for her desktop publishing expertise used in the layout of this publication.

xvi

1

Introduction

As a youth of sixteen I obtained my first employment with the United States General Land Office as a flunky doing survey work. We were on the west side of the Rio Grande, between Los Alamos, which at that time was a private boys' school, and San Ildefonso Pueblo. That was in 1927, during the summer months, and while there I crossed San Ildefonso Pueblo lands many times. Often I saw small groups of Indians out hunting rabbits with bows and arrows. As they were sometimes dressed in ceremonial garb, I now know that it was for a ritualistic occasion or purpose. Other times on our way to work we passed Indians driving teams and wagons on their way to the mesa tops which they dry-farmed during the summer.

In 1931 I was employed on a survey crew for the United States Geological Survey mapping the Rio Grande. It was during this time, when we mapped San Ildefonso Pueblo and Santa Clara Pueblo lands, that I began to develop an interest in the Indians and their arts and crafts—an interest which has continued to the present.

Lightning Dance , c. 1920. Museum of New Mexico Fine Arts Collection #3184.

     It was at this time also that I became good friends with another youth, Herbert Reiter, with whom I worked. He had an older brother, Paul, who was employed by the Museum of New Mexico at Santa Fe, working for Dr. Edgar Hewett, a professor of archaeology for the University of New Mexico and head of the School of American Research in Santa Fe. I spent a lot of time at the museum and thus increased my interest in all phases of Indian arts and crafts, including Indian paintings.

Making Pottery, c. 1918. Watercolor and ink. 14 1/2 x 22 1/2 inches. Museum of New Mexico Fine Arts Collection.

The paintings of the San Ildefonso group particularly fascinated me, my favorite works being those of Tonita Peña. I had no money to invest in paintings at that time and I have always regretted the lost opportunities to have done so. I never met Tonita personally but had many friends who knew her. As time went on, I accumulated an extensive library concerning the Southwest. Due to conflicting dates, quotations, and articles about the San Ildefonso artists, I decided to try and set the record straight for at least one of them and picked my favorite, Tonita Peña.

Undocumented dates of birth and confusion of relationships between individuals in many publications included in my research for this book led to the following format relating to dates: baptisms, marriages, and deaths recorded by day, month, and year have been verified directly from the

Eagle Dance, undated. Watercolor. 12 1/2 x 16 1/2 inches. Museum of New Mexico Fine Arts Collection #1272.

Catholic Church parish records. Quite often these church records clarified relationships between individuals which have long been confusing and sometimes erroneous.

When month and year only are given, they reflect statements from reliable informants, generally individuals who are related to the person in question. Dates given by the year only, or with a question mark, remain unsubstantiated.

Nearly all of the old Catholic Church parish record books of vital statistics are now stored in the Archdiocese Archives in Albuquerque, New Mexico. I found it extremely difficult to access these records, not only due to their fragile condition, but also due to the small research and clerical staff.

4

Buffalo Dance, c. 1935. Watercolor. 12 3/4 x 19 3/4 inches. Museum of New Mexico Fine Arts Collection.

Fortunately, The Church of Jesus Christ of Latter-Day Saints has recorded most of these records on 35mm tapes. I spent many hours studying these tapes and, although tedious, these hours were rewarding. Almost all of the old Catholic Church parish records were recorded by hand, using old-fashioned quill pens. The old priests were very proud of their penmanship and wrote with many flourishes. Also, their records were written either in archaic Spanish or in Latin. Unfortunately, I never became proficient in either of these, which made the translations much more difficult.

The United States Government Census records for New Mexico, which were first recorded in 1890, were destroyed by fire at some later date. The records dating from 1900 are available and have been studied. However, I found that they are generally unreliable, particularly in regard to the age of any individual. This became apparent when the same individual's age was

Buffalo Dance, undated. Watercolor. 10 1/2 x 15 inches. James T. Bialac Collection.
Photography by Jerry Jacka.

compared through different census periods. They have, nonetheless, been very valuable in the listing of household members of various families at the time of the census. Prior to the U.S. Census records, a census was taken by the Mexican government every ten years. However, these records did not include Indian families.

Extensive research was done by perusing books, periodicals, and manuscripts. I was fortunate to obtain statements from relatives, mutual friends, art collectors and dealers who knew Tonita personally.

2

A Pueblo Artist

Her Early Years at San Ildefonso Pueblo

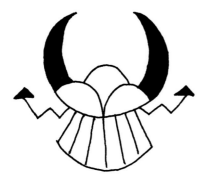

Maria Antonia Peña was born on May 10, 1893, in San Ildefonso Pueblo, to Ascencion Vigil Peña and her husband, Natividad Peña. At sunrise, four days after her birth, her godmother, Anastasia Peña from Tesuque Pueblo, took her outside at daybreak at San Ildefonso Pueblo to greet the Sun Father, as is pueblo custom, and named her Quah Ah, meaning Little Bead or Pink Shell, depending upon the informant.

After this ceremony, Quah Ah was baptized into the Catholic Church at San Ildefonso and recorded in the Peña Blanca church records as born on May 10, 1893 with the Spanish name of Maria Antonia Peña. Tonita had an older brother, Santiago Peña, and an older sister, Maria Alfonsa Peña. In 1899, Tonita's younger sister, Carañita Peña, was born.

Artistic ability was an inherited talent in Tonita's family background from her maternal side. Her maternal grandmother, Maria Tona (Arquero) Vigil was one of the older, well known potters of San Ildefonso when Tonita was born. Her grandfather, Juan Arquero, was born in Cochiti and had journeyed to San Ildefonso with a wagon load of yucca to sell; and while there, met, fell in love with, and married Tonita's grandmother.

The parish priest at San Ildefonso where they were married said that *Arquero* was not a proper Tewa name and so the priest changed Juan Arquero's name to Juan Vigil.

He continued to live in San Ildefonso the remainder of his life and raised a family of four children: Francisco Vigil, Alfonso Vigil, Martina Vigil, and Ascension Vigil (Tonita's mother). Tonita's uncle, Alfonso, was the father of Romando Vigil, Tonita's cousin who also became a famous painter.

Tonita's aunt, Martina Vigil, was a fine potter. According to Maria Martinez, she was the finest of the present-day (1895) potters. Martina's husband, Florentino Montoya, became a great painter of pottery. He learned pottery painting by occasionally painting his mother-in-law's pottery, even before Martina became well known as a potter. Florentino finally developed into one of the finest in the art of painting pottery as he painted all of Martina's work.

Florentino and Martina had made several trips from San Ildefonso to Cochiti before moving to Cochiti permanently. They made their first trip in 1901 when Florentino helped with the Cochiti harvest. Their frequent trips and final move were due to several unrelated circumstances. The fact that Martina's mother was from San Ildefonso and that her father was from Cochiti introduced into the Vigil family an old pueblo custom. Whenever inter-pueblo marriages occurred, the resulting family was considered to have responsibilities and fealties to both pueblos. This worked well as Florentino and Martina were very well liked and accepted in both pueblos.

Living in San Ildefonso Pueblo was a Navajo, Santiago Martinez. He and his sister were captured while quite young by a San Ildefonso raiding party into Navajo territory. The raiding party sold the baby girl to Mexicans as a slave but kept Santiago as a captive. He grew up to manhood and finally was accepted as a member of the pueblo. Santiago married Dominguita Pino and they had a son, Crescencio Martinez, who became one of the finest of the early San Ildefonso painters.

Florentino and Santiago became very good friends and the two families were the best of neighbors. No one seems to know why or how it happened, but Florentino and Santiago had a serious quarrel and disagree-

Matched large pots made by Tonita's aunt and uncle, Martina Vigil and Florentino Montoya.
c. 1905-1915, 20 1/2 inches high. School of American Research Collection.

ment. Their differences became so serious and polarized that it finally developed into violence. In fact, one day Santiago took his gun and shot through a window of his home at Florentino, but fortunately he missed. It happened to be witnessed by Dominguita's father who was standing outside his own house.

This unfortunate incident made any reconciliation quite impossible, so Florentino and Martina deemed it prudent to move to Cochiti. They had already been invited by the elders of Cochiti to come and make their home there. It is said that many of the people of San Ildefonso cried when Florentino gave up his tribal lands and moved to Cochiti, probably in 1903.

It is notable that when Florentino and Martina moved to Cochiti, Martina continued to use her San Ildefonso pottery shapes and style even though she was forced to adopt the use of Cochiti slip on her pottery. A slip on pottery consists of a very fine watery layer of clay applied to the exterior of the pot after the pot has air dried. It is used to smooth out little imperfections on the surface and is the base for painting designs on the pot before firing. Clay available in Cochiti was different from that Martina had been accustomed to using. With this slip the pottery was polished off with a rag instead of using the San Ildefonso technique of stone polishing. The resulting finish did not have the luster and sheen of San Ildefonso pottery, but had a dull, smooth finish.

Martina was influential in introducing the Cochiti slip to other San Ildefonso potters. This slip became popular with some of these potters as it did not require nearly so much work. Florentino continued to use his traditional San Ildefonso patterns in painting Martina's pots.

There was quite a lot of visiting between people of San Ildefonso and Cochiti and they usually exchanged gifts, generally pieces of pottery. One of the customs which became common as a result of this was that any pot given as a gift by an individual from either pueblo to a person from the other generally had some green applied as a dye or paint in the decoration after firing. This made it possible for people from either pueblo to preclude selling or re-giving the pottery by some other member of the family without the knowledge or consent of the original recipient. Kenneth Chapman puzzled over this phenomenon for years until Martina Vigil explained it to him.

Hopi Dance (Tomahawk), undated. Watercolor. 14 1/2 x 11 3/8 inches.
Museum of New Mexico Fine Arts Collection.

Quah Ah attended day school at San Ildefonso from about 1899 into 1905. According to Alice Corbin Henderson, Quah Ah credited Esther B. Hoyt, a San Ildefonso Day School teacher, with having first encouraged her and her sister, Alfonsonita, along with Alfredo Montoya, to paint in the pueblo day school. They started out using wax crayons for coloring. Miss Hoyt told the children to think of the dances in the plaza and of how they felt while dancing and to then paint or color what they thought. She never attempted to influence their style or technique.

Tonita said that Miss Hoyt used to bring her presents when she returned from vacations and that Miss Hoyt purchased some watercolor paintings by Tonita after giving her some watercolors.

It was at San Ildefonso that Edgar L. Hewett discovered Tonita and her talent. From that time on, he continued to furnish her with fine watercolor paints and paper and encouraged her to paint whatever came to her mind. Quite a few of these early paintings were of everyday life around the pueblo: grinding corn for meal, winnowing wheat, making pottery and painting it, and, of course, dancing. Later, her cousin Romando Vigil started learning art in the same way as Tonita, in day school. His teacher was Elizabeth Robbins.

There were several talented San Ildefonso artists in about the same time frame. All of these early painters came to be known as the San Ildefonso Movement or the San Ildefonso Self-Taught Group. Included in this group were Julian Martinez, Alfonso Roybal, Tonita Peña, Abel Sanchez, Crescencio Martinez, Encarnacion Peña, and others. Tonita was the only woman in this group and, as such, became the first pueblo woman Indian easel painter.

The Move to Cochiti Pueblo

In 1905, tragedy struck young Tonita. Her mother and little sister, Carañita, became ill and died in an influenza epidemic. Her older sister, Alfonsonita, had already married. Tonita's close and happy home life was completely shattered.

Her aunt and uncle, Martina and Florentino Montoya, had moved to Cochiti Pueblo by then. Tonita's father sorrowfully decided it was best to take her to Cochiti to live with her aunt and uncle so that she would not be home alone while he was busy working in the fields. It was a long way from

12

San Ildefonso to Cochiti, well over fifty miles, and it has been said that Tonita rode a burro from San Ildefonso to Cochiti while her father took her belongings in a wagon. The trip took two or three days. They probably stopped and spent the first night in Tesuque with her godmother, Anastasia. It was only about sixteen miles but it gave Tonita a chance to get used to riding the burro. Tonita and her father probably camped out the second night or spent the night at La Cienega, a little Spanish village above La Bajada (a tremendous drop down the twisting narrow road where it descends from the mesa plateau to the valley below, near the Rio Grande). The next day was all downhill from the mesa top and they crossed the Rio Grande to the pueblo of Cochiti along the west side of the Rio Grande.

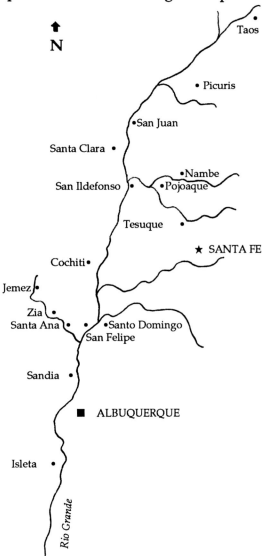

This family breakup and move, in addition to the death of her mother and sister, was a terrible heartbreak and burden to this twelve-year-old girl. Not only did she have to leave all her lifelong friends and neighbors, Tonita had to learn new customs, songs, and dances among strangers. She even had to learn a new language because the people at Cochiti spoke Keres while Tonita had always spoken Tewa.

It was fortunate that she was living with her Uncle Florentino and Aunt Martina, as they knew how to speak the

Black on red jar by Tonita, c. 1910. 9 x 11 1/2 inches. Collection of Marshall and Lucille Miller. Photography by The Photo Center, D. Roberts.

Keres language. Also, Tonita and her new friends could speak fluent Spanish, as well as some English.

The fact that she had her cherished paints helped to keep Tonita from becoming too homesick and lonely. At first she stayed close to home, learning the new language, helping her aunt with her pottery, and painting a lot. Since Tonita was a friendly and outgoing girl, it was not long before she acquired new friends and began to fit into the normal Cochiti Pueblo life. While in San Ildefonso, Tonita's Aunt Martina taught her to be a potter, while her grandmother and Uncle Florentino helped her learn the skill of painting pottery.

Even in San Ildefonso, Tonita used to help her Aunt Martina make the large ollas for water or storage jars with lids. Tonita's job was to keep the top edge of the huge jars moistened while her aunt prepared additional coils of

14

clay. If not kept wet, the unfinished top edge became too dry and the pot was sure to crack when fired. Tonita also helped in applying the slip and in polishing the large jars. Polishing required a great deal of time and patience and much tiring work, but it was fun to see the beautiful shapes develop. It was from Cochiti that Tonita entered St. Catherine's Indian School in Santa Fe. All of the school's enrollment records prior to 1920 were destroyed by a fire, so it is not known how long Tonita was a student.

Her Marriage to Juan Rosario Chavez

Tonita's Aunt Martina was slowly going blind from glaucoma, and her Uncle Florentino was getting very old. It was said that the elders of the pueblo decided it best if Tonita were to marry so that she would not be alone if her aunt and uncle died. They called Tonita back from school to the pueblo and arranged for her to be married.

The elders selected Juan Rosario Chavez to be Tonita's husband, so Juan and Tonita were married on March 2, 1908. Juan was twenty years old and Tonita was almost fifteen. On April 4, 1909 Juan and Tonita gave birth to a daughter, Helia Chavez.

These dates, including her birth as recorded in the church marriage records, correspond very closely with the Bureau of Census records. The San Ildefonso census records in 1900 show the following about Tonita's family:

Natividad Peña, farmer, head of household, age 35
Ascencionita Peña, housewife, age 35
Alfonsonita Peña, daughter, age 13
Tonita Peña, daughter, age 7
Carañita Peña, daughter, age 1
Santiago Peña, son, age 17

The census records for Cochiti in 1910 show:

Juan Rosario Chavez, farmer, age 20
Tonita Peña, housewife, age 18
Helia Chavez, daughter, age 1-1/2

On February 12, 1912 Tonita and Juan had a son they named Richard Chavez. Juan died after a short illness on May 17, 1912. Tonita did little painting during her marriage to Juan. After her husband's death, Tonita left her children with her Aunt Martina and returned to St. Catherine's, hoping to complete her schooling.

Her Marriage to Felipe Herrera

So that Tonita could be in Cochiti caring for her children as her aunt and uncle continued to get older, it was arranged that she marry again. On July 14, 1913 Tonita was married to Felipe Herrera. Felipe worked in the iron oxide mines at what is now the ghost town of Waldo on the Santa Fe Railway, just east of Cochiti.

When Tonita's Aunt Martina died in 1916, her Uncle Florentino returned to San Ildefonso. In 1917, after a trip to Flagstaff, he died of influenza. On May 17, 1920 Tonita and Felipe had a son whom they named Hilario J., now known as Joseph H. Herrera, a noted artist. A few months later, on July 16th, Felipe Herrera was killed in an accident at the iron oxide mine.

The marriage between Felipe and Tonita was a good one. Tonita had become very fond of him, especially after their son, Joe, was born. Her second husband's tragic death at the mine was another terrible blow.

Even though they were older than Tonita, Juan and Felipe were kind to her and very supportive of her ability as a painter. During the seven years she was married to Felipe, Tonita managed to finish her schooling at St. Catherine's Indian School and continued painting in her spare moments. Indicative of a good marriage, Tonita signed a few of her paintings Qua H. AH. (or Ah), rather than Quah AH, the H being separated from her Indian name, in tribute to her husband's name Herrera.

After Felipe's death, Tonita was kept busy with her children and with painting at Cochiti, ever under the watchful eye of Dr. Hewett, who continued to supply her with fine Winston brand watercolors from England and with good art paper. He also bought most of what Tonita produced for the Art Museum in Santa Fe until she became well enough known to provide for herself. When Dr. Hewett died, Tonita became a protege of Dr. Chapman, who also encouraged her in her artistic endeavors.

16

Eagle Dance, Cochiti, c. 1932. Watercolor. 7 1/2 x 11 1/2 inches. James T. Bialac Collection. Photography by Jerry Jacka.

Her Marriage to Epitacio Arquero

In the winter of 1921 Tonita met and fell in love with Epitacio Arquero. He had been a coal breaker at the mine in Waldo, but had returned to Cochiti to take up farming. On June 12, 1922 Tonita and Epitacio were married. She was twenty-nine and he was thirty-five. He was a farmer but was destined to become a very important man in the pueblo.

According to Charles H. Lange in *Cochiti* (see references), Epitacio became a *fiscale* in 1931 and 1932, a lieutenant war captain in 1937 (pueblo

17

Children of Tonita Peña, Cochiti Pueblo, c. 1934. Museum of New Mexico negative #134654.
Margaret (left) and Cerelia.

tribal offices), a governor in 1940, 1943, and 1944, and, after Tonita died in 1949, governor in 1951. He was a member of the Cochiti Council of Principales, another tribal office, in 1948, 1949, 1950, 1951, and 1952. Epitacio was also considered to be one of the finest drum makers in Cochiti Pueblo during his lifetime, and Cochiti was famous for its drums and drum makers.

Tonita became increasingly successful in her painting and her works were shown widely in museum exhibitions and in commercial art galleries in Santa Fe and Albuquerque, and were purchased by discerning art collectors. The large Fred Harvey hotel, La Fonda, on the southeast corner of the plaza in Santa Fe purchased a number of her paintings for display in the hotel rooms and suites.

Lange also noted that there had been little objection at Cochiti to Tonita's paintings of dance figures. However, there had been trouble during a year in which her third husband, Epitacio, was governor. It was thought by some that Tonita betrayed tribal secrets in some of her paintings. Her

Family of Tonita Peña, Cochiti Pueblo, c. 1934. Museum of New Mexico negative #134653. Seated (left to right), Margaret, Sam, and Epitacio. Standing, Cerelia (left), and Helia (right).

husband defended her by pointing out that since she was drawing only those dancers and dances which could be seen by any outsider, it was no more harmful for her to do this than it was for others to make decorated pottery and sell it. This reasoning apparently satisfied the objectors. After that Tonita resorted to painting Pueblo figures of an exoteric nature.

Tonita was completely enchanted in this loving and lasting marriage. She and Epitacio had five children. The first was Maria Cyrella, born on February 2, 1923; then came Virginia, born on December 15, 1924. They lost Virginia, not even two years old, on May 8, 1926. Margaretta was born on August 21, 1927; Sam was born on July 26, 1929; finally, Victoria, or "Vicki" as the family preferred to call her, was born on March 4, 1935. Thus, this gifted painter had eight children.

They were a very happy and caring family and Epitacio was a good father to them all. Tonita used to laugh and say "Pitacio, the best husband I ever had!" Tonita was busy being in charge of the home where her word was

19

law. Epitacio was boss in the fields. However, Tonita helped him with the farm work when necessary, especially during harvest. She was also a good neighbor to other ladies of the pueblo.

The Mature Years of Her Art

As they grew older, Tonita's older children helped a great deal with the babies, giving Tonita more time to indulge her desires for painting and selling her art. She also taught art at the Santa Fe Indian School and the Albuquerque Indian School.

Tonita's teaching was done in the traditional method of pottery making, painting of pottery, and other of the older art forms. It consisted of the show-and-tell method. Tonita would paint and the pupils would observe her technique and brush strokes. Then Tonita answered any of their questions.

Tonita both needed and wanted the money from painting because she was obsessed with several desires, all of which were expensive. She loved fine turquoise jewelry and had a beautiful collection. Tonita also enjoyed nice cars. There were always presents to be purchased for her children, grandchildren, and the many godchildren Tonita seemed to acquire. Whenever she returned from a selling trip to Santa Fe or Albuquerque, Tonita never failed to bring them all something.

Although it is said that the earliest paintings of the San Ildefonso Group never appeared until about 1914, Ida Fisher, who owned and operated an art gallery and frame shop in Albuquerque for many years, had several of Tonita's early paintings. She claimed to have acquired one or two of these painted as early as 1909, when Tonita was sixteen years old. They are signed but not dated, so Mrs. Fisher dated these old paintings by the type of paper upon which they were painted.

Prior to having her gallery on Central Avenue across from the University of New Mexico, the late Ida Fisher and her husband, also deceased, had a painting and art supply store near the university campus and supplied most of the fine art paper used in New Mexico. She claimed to be an expert in the identification and dating of art paper products. As Dr. Hewett and Dr.

20

Chapman both taught archaeology at the University of New Mexico, any art supplies they acquired during that period were probably purchased from the Fishers.

In an article "Art and Artists of New Mexico," *New Mexico Magazine*, November, 1933, Ina Sizer Cassidy says "The Indian artist is never troubled over the intellectual side of his art. He simply KNOWS his art and questions not.... And they do not confine their artistic expression to their watercolors and a piece of paper, either. I have watched Tonita Peña of Cochiti, for instance, with watercolors and virgin paper, absorbed in materializing her concepts of the ceremonial dances and I have watched her plastering the walls of her *adobe* home, small palms outspread smoothing the velvety brown mud over the surface with care and creative concentration. I have also watched her in the ceremonial dances in the *plaza*, her consecrated hands waving evergreen wands, rhythmically keeping time to the measured beat of the drum, and tread of her bare feet on the hot earth, and there is in all of these activities the same creative aesthetic quality which has made her one of the outstanding Indian painters of New Mexico, and I believe the only Indian woman to attain distinction in this newly revived expression.

"Tonita is delightfully modest over the success won in her few years of work in this new medium, and greets her friends today with the same sweet gentle dignity as before she became a celebrity. Tonita (Little Tony) Peña is her Spanish name; Quah Ah her more euphonious Indian one.

"In San Ildefonso when a visitor comes to the *pueblo* for the first time, the first person asked for is Marie, the potter, known over the world almost, for her fine pottery. In Cochiti in the same manner, Tonita is now being asked for, for she is rapidly becoming as well known as a painter as Marie is known as a potter."

Cassidy pointed out an outstanding example of Tonita's artistic ability on the portal of the James W. Young Rancho de la Cañada residence in Cochiti Canyon, northwest of Cochiti Pueblo. Quah Ah's painting is not actually a mural but is on the inner side of a heavy beam, an old bridge timber, which supports the vigas of the ranch house portal. This work, in oil, is about eighteen feet long, was completed in 1931, and retains the fresh appearance of the original oils. It depicts a series of Cochiti dancers and symbolic rain figures, with a wild-pigeon motif at either end. This house, together with the

Corn Dancer - Male, c. 1933. Watercolor. 7 x 5 1/2 inches.
Adobe Gallery. Photography by Focus Studio.

22

Corn Dancer - Female, c. 1933. Watercolor. 7 x 5 1/2 inches.
Adobe Gallery. Photography by Focus Studio.

Peter Rabbit dances the Eagle Dance. School Arts Magazine.

Peter Rabbit enacts the Corn Dance of the Pueblo Indian. School Arts Magazine.

accompanying ranch property, is now owned by the University of New Mexico.

Victoria Melchor, youngest daughter of Tonita, also told me about some unusual paintings which her mother did for her children. She painted small caricatures of bunny rabbits dressed up in Indian costumes. Victoria remarked that these charming bunnies were wonderful in teaching the various dances to the kids. Victoria said that, unfortunately, these small paintings were among the possessions of her mother when Tonita passed away. Following age-old tradition, upon her death, her husband, Epitacio, gathered

24

Peter Rabbit hunts for Easter eggs.
School Arts Magazine.

Peter Rabbit beats an Indian tom-tom.
School Arts Magazine.

Though the names on these are her children's, I have been assured that Tonita drew them .

all of Tonita's personal things, including paintings, from the home and placed them in an old shed nearby on their property and set fire to the building and destroyed all of the contents.

I had never seen or heard of these paintings, but Joe said he watched Tonita while she made these little pictures for the children, and that she drew similar ones using turtles and squirrels, confirming that they had, indeed, been made for all of the children of Tonita and Epitacio. While rummaging around in old boxes and piles of storage for some photographs of his mother, Joe came upon photocopies of a few of the drawings from an article in *School Arts Magazine,* published in 1945.

During the early 1930s Tonita, along with several other Indian artists, assisted in painting a series of murals under a WPA cultural project which hung in the Santa Fe Indian School dining hall. Some of them were later moved to the Albuquerque Indian School. Most of these large murals are now in private collections or in museums. Chester E. Faris, Superintendent from 1930 to 1935, donated three of these large murals to the Southwest Museum in Los Angeles in 1934. One of these was a mural by Tonita entitled "Hopi Basket Ceremony."

Tonita paints on canvas, Eagle Dance, c. 1935. Museum of New Mexico Fine Arts Collection negative #73945 (above), #73979 (right). Photography by T. Harmon Parkhurst.

Cochiti Pueblo Eagle Dancer, c. 1941. Watercolor. 7 x 6 inches.
School of American Research #P256.

27

Koshare, c.1930. Watercolor. 8 1/2 x 5 1/2 inches.
The Heard Museum, IAC #1534.

3

Personal Recollections
of Howard and Mike Shaw

I first met Howard Shaw in 1927 when we were both in high school in Santa Fe, New Mexico. During the summer months, when not in school, we both worked for the United States General Land Office on survey crews doing work on public lands.

Howard grew up in Santa Fe in a predominantly Spanish neighborhood. He attended the Catholic parochial school and then St. Michael's High School, also a Catholic institution, so Howard grew up speaking Spanish more fluently than English. In fact, he learned Spanish before he learned English. At some point, Howard dropped out of school; therefore, he spent more time than I working for the public survey. It was during this time, while working on a survey job around Quemado, New Mexico, that Howard met Ida Mae Curtis from Quemado. Ida Mae's father had nicknamed her "Mike," by which name she was most generally known. They married on July 1, 1934.

Ida Mae's father was Newton, Newt, or T.N., Curtis, a former state senator and prominent businessman in Catron County who owned extensive

29

ranch land and cattle and, at one time, leased from the state of New Mexico the land upon which was situated Salt Lake.

Salt Lake is a strange geological formation about fifteen miles northwest of Quemado. It is a rather small old volcanic cone surrounded by a lake. What makes it unique is that it has no outlet. With a rapid evaporating factor it is very high in salt content. Also, in the middle of the lake is a small, perfect volcanic cone from an eruption in the distant past. Inside the cone is more water which is much more salty than the surrounding lake.

Many tribes of Indians consider the lake sacred and have obtained salt for their use from it for generations down through the centuries. It was neutral ground for Indian tribes who normally were hostile with one another.

Nearby ranchers, at one time, obtained salt from it for their cattle. Shallow wooden boats were towed into the lake and wooden plugs in the bottoms were removed. When almost full, they were replugged and towed to shore. Here they were left to evaporate the water, leaving the salt which was then gathered in sacks.

Mr. Curtis permitted everyone the use of the lake for salt and allowed the Indians to hold their various ceremonies in connection with the gathering of their salt. Mr. Curtis finally let the lease on this state land lapse. The state continued to allow the lake to be used by everyone. However, at the present time, the lake has been deeded by the state to the Zuni Pueblo.

After Howard married, he continued to work for the U.S. General Land Office for several years. Eventually he acquired a state surveyor's license, became postmaster of Quemado, served a term in the New Mexico State Legislature, and helped with his in-laws' ranching and cattle activities.

When World War II started, Howard enlisted in the U.S. Air Corps. While in the service, by diligent study, he completed his high school studies, went into Officers' Training School, served throughout the war, and retired as a lieutenant colonel after twenty years of service.

After retiring, Howard and Mike went back to Quemado and built a new home. In 1972, Howard suffered a coronary occlusion and was confined to bed and wheelchair thereafter with round-the-clock nurses' care. Although his movements and speech were greatly impaired, Howard was just as alert and intelligent as ever. It was with deep regret and sorrow that I heard of Howard Shaw's death in midsummer of 1988.

Harvest Dance, undated. Watercolor. 13 x 22 inches. John and Barbara Juhl Collection. Photography by Focus Studio.

I returned from Kansas in 1959 and I visited Howard, also living in Albuquerque, frequently and enjoyed talking of old times together. In 1979 I told Howard that I was thinking of writing a book about the famous Indian painter, Tonita Peña. Imagine my astonishment when he exclaimed, "Why, I know her, she was my Indian mother!"

This chapter is the result of many, many hours of taping, transcribing, typing, and revising Howard's story. He tired easily and, due to his speech impairment, the task of obtaining this valuable information was staggering and required countless hours of effort. It not only documents the remarkable and beautiful relationship between Howard and Tonita, it also gives valuable ethnological insight into the everyday life of a typical pueblo Indian family as lived in the early 1900s.

Bow and Arrow Ceremony, Cochiti. Watercolor. 14 x 21 3/4 inches. Museum of New Mexico Fine Arts Collection, #1367-23P, negative #137340.

Howard K. Shaw's Early Years with Tonita Peña

I first knew Tonita and her husband, Epitacio Arquero, about 1924. They were friends of my mother and dad even before that. In about 1925 I used to go out and visit a friend at Cochiti, John Urban, half Mexican and half Cherokee Indian. John lived on a small ranch adjoining Cochiti Pueblo Reservation. He made a living by chasing, catching, and breaking wild horses, which he then sold. He also ran a small store in Cochiti Pueblo. As a youngster I was always fascinated with the Indians at the pueblo and hung around there every chance I had.

Through my folks I became friends with Tonita and her husband and I met their oldest son, Richard, who was about my own age. Gradually I

32

Negative #74039   *Negative # 74038*

Deer Mother Dancer performed only every three years on King's Day, January 6th. Undated. Museum of New Mexico Fine Arts Collection. Photography by T. Harmon Parkhurst.

began to spend more and more time at the pueblo, staying at Tonita's place. I spent a lot of time with Richard at every opportunity. Some summers I would spend a month or three weeks there. I remember one summer I spent a whole three months at the pueblo. As a result I became friends with most of the people there. I even spent some time there in the fall after I quit school.

Tonita's husband, Epitacio, and the rest of the family at that time, with the exception of Tonita, spoke only Keres, the Cochiti language, and Spanish. As a result we always talked in Spanish, especially Epitacio as he had never learned English. I never learned to speak the Keres language though I tried.

33

Tonita would introduce me to her friends and neighbors as her son, and I considered her my Indian mother. I always stayed at her home and was really considered one of the family. She never discussed her personal life with me so I never knew until later that Tonita had been married twice before and that Richard was a son by her first husband. As we always used first names only, I learned years later that Richard's last name was Chavez.

Tonita was always busy around the house, helping her husband, cooking, and helping her neighbors, but her paints were always out on a table and Tonita painted whenever she had some spare time. The older kids, mainly the girls, took care of the younger ones so that Tonita did not have to spend too much time with them and she used that time in painting.

Sometimes, I used to go over to the home of an Indian friend by the name of Joe Trujillo and play cards with him. He loved to play a card game called Coon-Can. He had a harelip. He only had one chair, I remember, so he always pulled out an old rawhide-covered trunk for me to sit on. Then we would play cards. One time I asked him, "Joe, what in the hell have you got in that trunk?" He didn't say anything until we finished the game.

Then he said "Come over here" and he lifted up the lid of the trunk and it was full of money, bills of all denominations! As it turned out, Joe was the pueblo treasurer. I said, "Doesn't it bother you with a bunch of kids running around here and you having so much money lying around in the house?" "No," he said, laughing. "Nobody will bother me. Nobody in the pueblo would come and take it, so all I have to worry about is some outsider or stranger and, then, if anything like that would happen, I would grab my rifle and shoot them." Then I said, "I am a stranger," and Joe replied "You are no stranger anymore and I know you, and I know that Tonita and Epitacio would not have you around if you were that kind of boy." I never did tell anybody about the money because I sure didn't want to get shot.

Tonita's house was always spotless and I remember one day while I was sitting on the floor that it looked clean enough to eat from. The board floors were bleached white and were smooth from so much scrubbing.

Epitacio's farm was down on the other side of the river where it was lower and they could irrigate. They raised squash, beans, corn, cabbage, watermelon, cantaloupe, and another melon they called muskmelon. They also grew chile. They had very little fresh meat unless someone killed a rabbit

34

Deer Dance, c. 1925-30. Opaque paint on thin board. 9 1/2 x 14 inches. Elkus Collection, Department of Anthropology, California Academy of Sciences.

or a deer. As a youngster I don't remember any turkeys or chickens in the pueblo, although they had them later when I was grown up and visited Tonita and Epitacio.

The meals we had were generally simple fare. For breakfast we would have pancakes once in a while with syrup; sometimes it would be posole and tortillas; sometimes we would have piki bread and use it as corn flakes with canned milk. We never had fresh milk because, you see, we had no refrigeration or electricity at the pueblo. Chile was on the table all the time and you could have it at any meal. Once in a while we would have eggs. They would buy them at Joe Urban's store there in Cochiti. Other times we would have tortillas and beans. They would put green beans in a pan of water and boil them with a little lard. Squash was baked. Cabbage was boiled like green

Untitled, undated. Watercolor. 14 x 22 1/2 inches. Collection of Howard H. Huston.

beans. After the beans were ripe they were shelled, dried, cooked the way the Mexicans cooked them, and called *frijoles*.

On a Feast Day the young people would get together in groups, put oilcloths on the floors of the houses and put big bowls of beans and chile, posole, and tamales rolled round in corn husks, and lots of melons on the oil-cloths. Richard and I would go from house to house and, boy, some of that food was absolutely out of this world!

Back when I was younger, visiting the pueblo before the Cochiti Dam was built by the U.S. Government for flood control, they had a wooden bridge across the river. Now they have a concrete bridge and asphalt roads. The east side of the river was lower than the pueblo, and flat, and each family had a piece of land where they could irrigate and farm. The men did all of the farming and would be gone all day. Everyone had horses and wagons which they used in farming, hauling wood, and for traveling. Nobody had cars in those days at the pueblo.

36

Untitled (Buffalo Dance), undated. Watercolor. 11 x 16 inches. Collection of Jack Sellner.

One time when I was out there in the fall I got to help Epitacio harvest the corn. We pulled the corn from the stalks while the husk was still green and, when the wagon was loaded, we would go back to the house. Tonita, early that morning, would have built a big fire in the *horno,* an outside oven built of adobe in the shape of a bee hive, and kept it fired all day.

When we got back with the corn, Tonita would rake out the fire and coals and it was sure hot. Before it got dark we put the whole wagon load of corn in that oven with the husk still on. There weren't any Spanish people who cooked corn that way. I don't know how many times we would fill the horno that way. The next morning we would go out and Tonita would pull the door off the front of the oven and, oh, it was still hot! She would pull out the corn and let it lie on the ground a little while to let it cool.

When it got cool enough to handle, we would pick up an ear and pull down the shuck on one side and then the opposite side, and hand them to Tonita. She would take the ears of the corn and tie the husks together so that they hung from the clothesline. When they were cold and dry they were stored for the winter. The cornstalks were then cut, hauled across the river, and piled on top of one of the storage sheds for winter feed for the horses.

Every time I went to the pueblo in those days, it seemed to me that Epitacio and I had to go after wood. We would get cedar and piñon. I don't know how many wagon loads of wood I helped him cut and haul in. It seemed to me that the family would use almost a cord every day. Also, it got to where you had to go quite a way from the pueblo to get wood. Every house burned wood in the winter to keep warm; they used it in the outside oven to bake bread and to prepare the corn, and also in the cook stove or in the fireplace to keep warm.

Tonita baked bread in the horno at least once a week. Her freshly baked bread, while still warm, was the best bread in the world. She would take the rolls of bread dough and roll them in a damp white cloth to keep them till baking time. Then she would unwrap them and put them in the oven for baking. Tortillas she would make on top of the stove and piki bread she would make on a piki stone.

This was a large stone, very smooth and flat, which was heated over an open fire. The watery, creamy corn meal was poured upon the hot stone and cooked very thin, like paper. I called it paper bread. It was really the first corn flakes when it was crushed and eaten in a bowl with milk. Tonita was noted for making the best piki bread in the pueblo.

I was talking to Tonita one day while she was painting and she turned to me and said, "I have received a letter and it said that some of my paintings are on display in Paris." Then she asked me, "Where is Paris?" I said, "Paris is in France. France is a country on the other side of the Atlantic Ocean from us and Paris is the capital." She said, "How far is that?" I said, "I'd judge around seven thousand miles." She looked at me as if she did not comprehend something that far away. So, I said, "Well, Tonita, the best way I can explain that to you is that from Cochiti to Albuquerque is fifty miles. Paris, France is as far as going from Cochiti to Albuquerque and returning back to Cochiti, and if you did that as many as one hundred times, you would then know how far it is to Paris, France." She said, "Oh, my, that's a long way!"

One time when I was fairly young, we were all sitting around in the large living room in the evening. This was one of the times that it was customary for Epitacio to give lessons to the little children about the songs and dances they needed to learn for the many ceremonies. Hanging in this room was a large drum which had been in the family for many years. The original heads were not on the drum then as they had to be replaced about every twenty years. Constant use of the drum and countless ceremonies would gradually wear out the heads but the original drum body was still intact.

Epitacio would take the drum down on those evenings and beat it and teach the kids the songs and dances. He was very particular that they learn everything just perfectly. Epitacio was considered to be the best drum maker in the Cochiti Pueblo, and Cochiti drums are the best made by all of the pueblos.

After many of these evenings, I finally learned to pick up the beat of the drum for the various dances. Epitacio would let me beat the drum and he would concentrate all of his time teaching the children the songs and dances for the different ceremonies.

As I have said previously, Tonita had told everybody in the pueblo that I was her son, and almost every time she would invite me to come to the pueblo for a visit, it seemed they would have a game of *pelota*, something like field hockey or shinny.

Before the game, Epitacio and I would take the horses and wagon and drive up near the mountains and he would always take along a shovel and an ax. He would finally find the bush he was looking for, what we call buckbrush. Epitacio would then select a single stem about as big as my middle finger, take the shovel, and dig it up. On the bottom end would be a kind of club-root, like a ball. He would take the ax and cut the stem about three feet long and, when it was all cleaned up, it looked something like a golf club. We would gather several of these clubs to use in the game.

The playing field was the plaza at the pueblo and the game was always between the Elders and the Juniors. The Elders were the men whose ages were forty and over, even up to eighty, and the Juniors were all under forty. The ball was homemade and covered with rawhide.

One time, during a game, I had the ball and I was running as fast as I could, and, boy, I was going to score when out of the corner of my eye, I saw something coming up fast and there was a man, an elderly man. He was seventy-five years old, but he took the ball away from me, went back the other way with it and scored a goal! Those older men were fast and tough. They didn't get older, just faster and tougher.

Another time, when I was at the pueblo, they had a rabbit hunt where it seemed as if everyone in the pueblo participated. Epitacio and I went back to the mountains and found some more buck-brush. We dug it up the same way as before, but this time we cut the handles about eighteen inches long. We got enough so that we each had two to use in the hunt.

All of the men formed a line where we were to hunt and the line was about one hundred yards long. The women were in back of the men with the wagons. Each woman had a shovel. We would hold one club in our right hand and carry the other in our left hand. If a rabbit jumped up, all you had with which to kill the rabbit was the club in your hand. If the rabbit ran down a hole, the women behind us would grab a shovel and dig down in the hole. It was never very deep and when the rabbit jumped out you had to hit it over the head with the club. They killed wood rats, what we call pack-rats, the same way.

So, on this hunt, I killed one wood rat and one cottontail rabbit. Epitacio got two wood rats and one cottontail. Every time we killed something, Tonita would run up and take it back to the wagon where she would skin it, clean it out, and throw it into a big pan in the back of the wagon.

Somewhere we got another wood rat because when we got back to the house we had four wood rats and two cottontails. Tonita washed all of the game, tied a string around each one's hind feet, and hung them on nails behind the cook stove. With a fire in the cook stove they dried very quickly and the meat did not spoil.

So every morning, before I ate breakfast, I would take a peek down the line and count the rats. One morning I was late for breakfast and, boy, was I hungry. We had posole with some meat and it was delicious. Then I remembered to check the rats and two were gone! And that is how I found out that wood rats are good to eat.

One summer day Tonita was painting and I was sitting in the sun in the doorway and talking to her. We were talking about all the different pueblos up and down the Rio Grande and I asked her, "Tonita, why are there so many pueblos and why don't they all live in one big pueblo?" She quit

40

12 1/2 x 14 inches
Catalog #192c.

8 x 7 1/2 inches.
Catalog #192a.

9 1/2 x/ 13 inches.
Catalog #192b.

13 x 20 inches.
Catalog #192d.

Paintings of Cochiti pottery, c. 1940. Watercolor. School of American Research Collection, catalog #192.

painting and started cleaning her brushes—she seemed to be wondering if she should tell a non-Indian the story, and then she began.

Many hundreds of years ago, all of the pueblo Indians lived in one great communal pueblo which was on the Pecos River and was called Pecos Pueblo. It is now abandoned and in ruins. All of the people were perfectly content, making pottery, raising families, and farming along the fertile Pecos River valley. Due to the fact that they engaged in no warfare with one another and that the Plains Indians had not molested them for years, the population outgrew the living capacity of the farms, and there became a shortage of fields to feed so many people. The Pueblo Council of Elders gathered in their kivas and discussed the various plans to remedy this alarming condition. One of the wisest elders came up with this plan: it would be best for all to continue to live together. He would take the first boy born in the pueblo after the meetings and, through his magic power, transform the child into a sacred snake. Another kiva would then be built for the home of this sacred snake.

From that time on, every first born child of every family would be fed to the sacred snake and the snake, by his magical powers, would provide for all of the needs of the people.

All of this was agreed upon and the snake was created. The kiva was built and the sacred snake was moved into his new kiva. Everything happened as was foretold and the people had plenty to eat and prospered and were happy. After the passing of many years, the snake grew to such an enormous size that it required more children than were originally agreed upon to satisfy its gluttonous appetite. The people dared not refuse the snake because he threatened to destroy their livelihood. The needs of the snake caused the population to decrease alarmingly and the people decided it seemed wise to get rid of the sacred snake. Such drastic measures were not to be undertaken lightly. So, one day all of the people gathered in the plaza beside the snake's kiva to decide what was best to be done. After much discussion, it was decided that the best solution would be to leave their mother pueblo as they dared not stay with the snake. They would search for other homesites away from the snake. Many left the next day in panic and others soon followed. Some of them went across the mountains and started Nambe Pueblo. Others, following the

42

Basket Dance, undated. Tempera. 13 1/8 x 18 7/8 inches. Museum of New Mexico Fine Arts Collection #1552.

Rio Grande, established many pueblos up and down its banks. Soon, Pecos Pueblo was deserted.

Legend says that the Cochiti group, one of the first to leave Pecos, settled in Frijoles Canyon and lived in cliff dwellings, and that these people are the ancestors of the present Cochiti Pueblo. The San Juan and Santa Clara groups started the Puye cliff dwellings and lived there until they moved down by the Rio Grande for better farming after a prolonged and severe drought.

The sacred snake had listened to all of this talk and heard the people leaving. He was remorseful, but also very angry, so, during the night, he broke out of his kiva and hid. The next morning the remaining people of the pueblo trailed the serpent to a cavern that is now known as Pecos Cave. This cave has a small opening on the south side of Lake Peak in the Sangre de Cristo Mountains at an elevation of about twelve thousand feet. It has been said that the cave has been partially explored by local people who have gone into the

Buffalo Dance, c. 1926. Watercolor. 10 1/2 x 15 inches. James T. Bialac Collection. Photography by Jerry Jacka.

interior of the cavern for about two miles at which point the cave is slashed by a deep chasm which they believe to be bottomless. The Indians say that this chasm was created by the tears of the snake while running away. Later, the tears dried up, leaving an impassable dry canyon. It is also believed that there is another opening to this cave on the north side of Lake Peak near Nambe Pueblo.

The Indians believe that the snake is still in the cave and it is said that every year twelve Indian men from Nambe Pueblo go into the cave on the Nambe side and stay three days, and that only eleven men come out.

44

Tonita spent every bit of her free time painting and I believe that painting was her life. I never saw her do any pottery-making although she made and gave one to my mother and father, which we still have. My parents also had a lot of Tonita's paintings, but they all disappeared when they died, while I was still in the service.

One fall, Epitacio and I went deer hunting. We took the horses and wagon towards the mountains west of Cochiti as close as we could get to where we wanted to hunt. We just parked the wagon there for a while. We left the wagon and were running side by side when, all of a sudden, in front of us jumped out four does and Epitacio killed all of them. I was almost scared to death as I was sure that the game warden would come around somewhere, somehow. I tried to push him back but he wouldn't pay any attention. Epitacio just said, "No, no, no..." and kept shooting.

When I got down to where the deer had fallen, I looked to see what Epitacio was doing. He had a little buckskin bag, no larger than your thumb, and it had a thong on it and he wore it around his neck. He pulled that thing out and got something out of it. It looked like corn meal to me. He sprinkled blood on one doe's head and then some corn meal and he said something in the Keres language. He went to each deer and did the same thing and when I kept looking at him he said, "Look, *es negocio de Indio*," which translates into English as, "This is Indian business." I took his word for it.

We got the deer all skinned and gutted and Epitacio took one of the stomachs, turned it wrong side out, and cleaned it in a nearby snowbank. He then turned it right side out again and scooped up the blood from one of the doe's cavities. He filled the stomach with blood and tied up the openings. I kept looking at him and asked him about this blood and he finally grinned and said, "*Sangre de venado esta muy bueno por el corazon.*" Translated, it means that "deer's blood is good for heart trouble."

We carried the blood and the deer down to the wagon and we took it all down to the pueblo where he dressed the deer out and cut them up. Epitacio told me that we would spread this blood out thin, about as thin as a silver dollar, and let it dry. As it dries, you can break it up and put it in a jar where it will keep. He said, "If you break off a piece of this as big as a nickel and put it in a half-full glass of water, when it is dissolved, drink it, and it is

45

Pottery bowl made by Tonita. 11 3/8 inches diameter by 7 inches deep. Personal collection of Mrs. Howard K. Shaw. Photography by Focus Studio.

good medicine for heart trouble." Years later I found out that he was getting this blood for Richard because he had heart trouble.

Another time Epitacio took me into his kiva to show me the kiva and talk to some of the elders who were there. All I saw was a big, circular room with a bench, or seat, all around the inside wall of the kiva, for the elders to sit on. Epitacio told me that I was the only white man ever to be in his kiva and I considered that to be a great honor.

Sometimes Richard and I would take our horses and just roam the mountains. Back where the mesas run into the Jemez Mountains, the pine

46

Untitled, c. 1940. Watercolor. 15 x 22 inches. Museum of Northern Arizona, negative #77-0438.

forest begins. You have these great western yellow pines, some as big as five or six feet in diameter. Then there would be open parks or glades where the bluegrass grows belly deep to a horse. These might be fringed with large aspen groves sometimes so thick you couldn't ride a horse through.

Before we would go on one of these expeditions, Tonita would make up a stack of tortillas about eighteen inches high. She would fry them lightly in oil and that kept them from getting dry and hard. We would put them in a flour sack and tie them on behind one of the saddles. Then she would make jerky with parched corn and we would tie that one behind the other saddle. We each carried .22-caliber rifles in saddle scabbards so we could shoot a rabbit sometimes and roast it over the campfire at night. We also carried our blankets behind the saddles.

Boy, those were great days, just going no particular place at all, and actually as free as a bird! Time meant nothing to us and we would roam around until we ran short of food and then go back to the pueblo. One time

47

we rode over to the north to see the stone lions south of Frijoles Canyon. No one knows how long they have been there, but they were probably carved by the ancestors of the Cochiti as a shrine. Sometimes we would find the big cactus fruit, ripe, and we would knock the red fruit, about the size of a golf ball, off the plant. We would sharpen a small stick and put it in the end of the fruit. Using this as a handle, we could then hold the fruit by the stick and carefully, with a knife, peel the skin and stickers off. The inside was creamy white with tiny black seeds that had the most delicious flavor. We ran into a lot of things like that just riding along game trails. I would love to be able to go back there and try to find some of that cactus.

Mike Reminisces about Tonita

The first time I ever met Tonita was shortly after Howard and I were married. We were living at Howard's parents' house in 1934 and it was during Fiesta week in September. We had been down to Quemado, which is where I was raised, and arrived in Santa Fe one evening and went right to bed.

The next morning, when I got up, I wandered into the living room and bowed out hurriedly because there was one Indian after another, rolled up in blankets sleeping on the floor. The room was full of Indians. There must have been about nine of them. I was a little frightened and rushed back into our bedroom, woke Howard, and said, "What in the world is going on in the living room?" "Oh," he said, "That's just Tonita and her family. They always stay here when they come to Santa Fe."

That was the way I met Tonita. The rest of the Indians evaporated when the introductions were over in the morning. They came and went erratically. You'd never know when they'd be in the house. But Tonita stayed at the house most of the time. Sometimes when she brought some paintings to sell, she would be gone, visiting the art galleries and various regular customers and other friends. She washed and ironed her apron every day and shampooed her hair every day also. We got to be good friends, visiting every day around the house and I became very fond of Tonita. I always thought that her paintings were beautiful.

And then, on our first visit to Cochiti at her home, she presented me with a beautiful Hopi wedding sash which I cherish to this day. Every time

Left to right: Epitacio Arquero, Joe Herrera, Jr. (Tonita's grandson), Tonita Peña, and Howard K. Shaw.

we went to Quemado or back we would stop off, if even for an hour, to visit her and Epitacio.

A short time later, Tonita and Epitacio came to Santa Fe and, as usual, we found them sleeping on the living room floor. I can't remember if it was that day or the next that Epitacio disappeared. Tonita stayed, washed and ironed her apron, and shampooed her hair as she always did. She stayed for a day or two, not mentioning Epitacio's absence as anything unusual. I missed Epitacio but, being recently married and things of this nature being new to me, I didn't question anyone too much in Howard's family. Then one day, around mid-morning, Epitacio showed up.

I was gone from the house for a while and, when I came in, I saw that Epitacio was sitting by Tonita in the living room, his head hung low. None of Howard's family was present at the time and we three were alone in the home. Tonita, in her very formal, quiet little manner, was sitting sort of diagonally facing him, and she, for thirty minutes or an hour, was talking to him. She must have been speaking to him in Keres because I couldn't understand a word. I thought she was doing some kind of a chant or something. It went on and on and I retired from the room.

Presently, Howard came in and went back to the kitchen. I followed him into the kitchen and said, "What's going on in there?" "Well," Howard replied, "she's really letting Epitacio have it because Epitacio got drunk and he ran back to the pueblo." It was about twenty miles across the mountains, a fast trip from what I understand. By the time Epitacio arrived at the pueblo he had sobered up and jogged back to our house. She was really letting him have it, which was interesting to me. Tonita, in her quiet little voice and that nice calm demeanor, was scolding him, and this great big guy, with his head hung, wasn't saying a word.

When we came back from Germany, Howard was still in the military service. We were staying in Quemado at my mother's house and we decided to go to Santa Fe. As usual, we planned on stopping off at Cochiti to see Tonita. I had always wanted my mother to meet Tonita so we took my mother along to meet her. My mother didn't care too much for Indians. All she had ever seen of Indians were some from around Reserve, New Mexico. They were inclined to be dirty and heavy drinking was prevalent. We finally talked her into going with us and, to tell the truth, mother had heard so much from us about this wonderful woman that I think she was downright curious.

When we arrived at Cochiti, we drove to her home, pulled up in the drive close to the house, and stopped. We got out of the car and there came Tonita, running. She and Howard embraced. Then she threw her arms around me and hugged me. I said, "Tonita, I'd like you to meet my mother, Mrs. Curtis." So, in a very formal way, Tonita walked up to my mother, took her hand and shook it, and said, "I am very happy to meet the mother of my daughter-in-law." We then went into the house and enjoyed a nice, leisurely, two-hour visit and lunch and, to be frank, my mother was completely enchanted with this lovely, gentle woman.

That was the last time we visited with Tonita. We were saddened to hear of her death in 1949 while Howard was still in the service and out of the States.

4

Personal Recollections
of Pablita Velarde

Pablita Velarde was born in 1918 at the Pueblo of Santa Clara, about twenty-eight miles north of Santa Fe. She was given the name Tse Tsan, Golden Dawn in the Tewa language of her people.

During early childhood, Pablita attended St. Catherine's Mission School at Santa Fe where she first learned English. At seventeen, she was graduated from Santa Fe Indian School.

While there Pablita had studied art under the direction of Dorothy Dunn, pioneer instructor of many now-famous Indian artists.

While in school, Tonita introduced Pablita to the magical world of art. Through this friendship Pablita became very interested in interpreting the proud and ancient traditions of her people.

I spent a delightful luncheon and a good part of one afternoon with Pablita talking about her early childhood and the enormous impact on her art from her friendship with Tonita. Pablita first met Tonita at Santa Fe Indian School, where Tonita was working with the group of original self-taught artists, who were mostly from San Ildefonso, including Romando Vigil (Tonita's cousin), Alfredo Montoya, Fred Kabotie (Hopi), and others who

51

were painting a number of large murals for Santa Fe Indian School. These murals were later exhibited all over the United States. Some were finally moved to the Albuquerque Indian School but now seem to have disappeared. No one knows whether they were discarded or stolen.

Tonita was staying at the women's dormitory at the school and, when not working on the murals, she would do her own paintings in her dormitory room. Pablita would visit with Tonita, and learn a lot just by being a looker and by asking questions. They both spoke Spanish, a language common to Santa Clara and San Ildefonso pueblos.

Once when Pablita asked Tonita why she liked to paint during all of her spare moments, Tonita laughed and said, "Well, it's better than washing clothes, or taking care of children, or fighting with my husband." Pablita said Tonita was always joking or teasing; that she was a very pleasant woman with whom to talk and spend time.

Pablita said, "Tonita had a happy personality and always showed that she felt good and satisfied with her life. I used to call her my aunt and she liked that. She was not really my aunt; but in Indian ways, anyone older was an aunt to me. Actually, she was. I might put it my own way and say she was kind of a mother figure to me, as I lost my own mother when I was quite young."

Tonita said that while still in day-school, a man named Dr. Hewett saw some of her art work, gave her watercolor paints and paper, and told her to draw and color dance figures or whatever she wanted. Tonita told Pablita, "I drew little figures and he liked them so I drew lots of them. I painted pictures of everything that I could think of. I don't know what he did with them, but anyway he paid me money for them and kept me in paint and paper." She never told Pablita how much Dr. Hewett paid her, but Pablita said that she was eventually making a small income from it, even while quite young.

Pablita had always wanted to paint, even when she was thirteen or fourteen, and she asked Tonita how to get started. Pablita said she had become tired of just work, work, work around the house; just gardening, housecleaning, and other woman's work. She was constantly dreaming of painting but did not have the nerve to start or did not know how to begin. It seemed to be inside her, all bottled up.

52

Navajo Dance, 1920. Watercolor. 14 x 22 inches. New Mexico Museum of Fine Arts Collection, #1048.

Tonita said, "I really don't know how I got started, except I just felt like I had to do it, so I did. It seemed that, at first, nobody seemed to care what I was doing anyway. Then people seemed to like what I was doing."

Pablita said that she just watched Tonita paint and tried to remember as best she could what Tonita talked about when she discussed colors and how she used the different brush strokes. Then Pablita would get out her own paints to try painting herself. She studied art later under Dorothy Dunn at Santa Fe Indian School, but told me that she would never have had the courage to start without first having the encouragement, help, and friendship of Tonita Peña.

Tonita and Pablita used to go together to display their art under the portal at the Palace of the Governors located on the north side of the plaza in

San Ildefonso Comanche Dance, c. 1942. Watercolor. 10 3/4 x 13 3/4 inches. The Amerind Foundation, Dragoon, AZ, #1666.

Santa Fe. Here they joined all the other Indians who displayed their pottery, jewelry, paintings, rugs, and other handiwork for sale to the tourist trade. It was a good place to do business because one did not need a license and could sell cheaper than the stores because those stores had to buy from the Indians who made the arts and crafts. The city never charged the Indians a fee or tax for selling under the portal because it helped to attract more tourists, who contributed significantly to the economy.

The two women set up their paintings side by side under the portal and, when business was slack, gossiped and compared notes. Tonita would tease Pablita and call her a looker, trying to steal some of her ideas. Pablita would then tell Tonita that she had no competition from her, an amateur trying to get started, while Tonita was already a well-known professional artist.

Cochiti Pueblo Eagle Dance, undated. Watercolor. 11 1/4 x 14 1/4 inches. School of American Research #P125.

Pablita told me that Tonita was quite a woman. She seemed to be always carefree and seemed to have met and married men who were very supportive and understanding of her need to be an artist. Pablita said that such support and encouragement are so hard to get when you are a woman and want to be married—that a husband may resent your career. She said that then you can't paint, and you get very unhappy about your life and become frustrated and depressed. This is one of the reasons that Pablita's marriage finally ended in divorce. From this marriage Pablita had a son and a daughter. Her daughter, Helen Hardin, who also became a very well-known artist, died unexpectedly in 1984, which was a terrible blow to Pablita.

"I never could understand how Tonita could have all those children, run a home, help her husband with crops, and still have time to do so many

Cochiti Pueblo Dancers, c. 1920s. Watercolor. 11 x 13 inches. School of American Research #P126.

paintings." Pablita said that in addition to those activities during the thirties, Tonita was always in demand in either Albuquerque or Santa Fe, to paint, teach, sell paintings, or do work for the museums. The oldest of her daughters, Helia, took care of the younger children and they made out all right. In those days, the men's only work was farming so they were gone from the home most of the day, leaving the older girls, or possibly an aunt or cousin, to help with little ones.

I asked Pablita if she remembered Romando's sister, Lena, the mother of Blue Corn, the wonderful potter. Lena died of tuberculosis when she was only eighteen or nineteen years old. Pablita had not known her, but said that her own mother also died young of the same disease. There was no doctor in the pueblo to tell how to take care of it, and many Indians contracted the disease.

After her mother died, Pablita's father would take all of his children up on the mesas beyond the Puye ruins in the summer and dry-farm the mesa tops where there was a lot of fresh air. Her father said that was one of the remedies the doctors used to cure tuberculosis. It must have worked because neither Pablita nor any of her brothers or sisters contracted tuberculosis. Pablita said that in later years she developed asthma, but that it never bothered her except when she would become upset or when there was a change in the weather. I asked Pablita if her mother had ever made pottery and she replied, "I don't know, as I never knew my mom, but my grandmother, Qualupita Sisneros, made pottery, and my sisters all took after my grandma and made pottery." For some reason she does not know, Pablita's father was also born a Sisneros, but early in life was given to a Velarde family to raise. When he started school, Velarde was the name by which the school recorded him. Pablita does not know where the name Velarde came from as those kinds of records were not kept during those times.

Pablita says that she always gave Tonita credit for being the first pueblo woman Indian to paint using watercolor on paper. She said, "There was no way that I or any other Indian artist could steal that title from Tonita because she was the only Indian woman artist I knew or heard of when I was young, and she helped me learn to paint. She was from that first group that was self-taught."

Straight Dance, 1919. Watercolor. 12 x 18 inches. James T. Bialac Collection.
Photography by Jerry Jacka.

5

Personal Recollections
of Her Children

Tonita's son

The following remarks about Tonita Peña were by her son, Joe Herrera, while reminiscing about his childhood days. They demonstrate the loving, caring atmosphere Tonita always seemed to create around her home:

"It was my job, when my mother was painting during the summer, to stand guard and swat the flies away to keep them out of the paint. They seemed to particularly like the yellows and the blues because they were sweet. How did I know they were sweet? I tasted them! When she had only a little paint left in a tube, she would give it to me and I would go over in a corner and practice my own painting. I seemed to have inherited my mother's talent as an artist and she never failed to encourage me in my early attempts.

"One time when I must have been about five or six, I was playing with a bunch of the neighbor boys and we found a hen's nest in a hole in a haystack. Being the smallest I was delegated to crawl into the nest and gather the eggs. We then divided them up among us and the other boys took theirs down to the store and traded them for candy. I took mine home and it didn't take long

59

Tonita at work, c. 1942. Photograph from Joe H. Herrera.

for mother to learn the whole story. After softly lecturing me about the evils of stealing, her punishment was swift and effective. After making sure that no one was looking, she took one of the eggs and whacked me on the forehead, smashing it, and made me return the others to the rightful owners with egg on my face."

According to Joe, Tonita told him that she used herself as a model for the face or faces in her early paintings of women. He also said that her paintings of pottery were copies of pots that she herself had made and decorated.

Joe went to the Santa Fe Indian School and was graduated in 1940, and then served in the United States Army, stationed mostly in Puerto Rico, until the end of World War II. After the end of the war, he attended the University of New Mexico in Albuquerque on the G.I. Bill and acquired his Master of Arts degree in art.

In letters to his Santa Fe friends during his war years, Joe always referred to his mother as "my sweetheart mother."

Tonita's daughter

The following letter was written to me by Victoria Melchor, Tonita's youngest daughter, who lives in California, in reply to my request for personal remembrances concerning pueblo life, especially in relation to her mother. I consider her answer a very fitting and beautiful addition to Tonita Peña's life story:

Dear Mr. Gray:

I would like to thank you for writing to inform me that you are working on mother's biography. I am very excited about it and will be looking forward to its publication.

Your letter was received with much appreciation and it is most satisfying to know that, finally, the beautiful life of my mother will be told. I feel that by reading about her life, many might feel inspired, as she has been to me. Mother was a unique lady, with so much love for her people and the Indian Arts. She used her creative talents and energies in so many ways to express this love. She had such a tremendous energy. She was always doing something for her family or for others. Not only did she paint to help support her family, but she also did a great deal to help other young beginning painters.

Making Tissue Bread, 1918. Watercolor. 14 1/4 x 22 1/2 inches. New Mexico Museum of Fine Arts Collection, #73650.

Since her culture meant a great deal to her, she helped with community affairs as much as she could. Along with all of that, she was right there along with my father, the late Epitacio Arquero, helping him with the planting and harvesting of grains, vegetables or fruits. She also had a lovely flower garden, all around the front of our house, which she tenderly cared for. She made our house the prettiest house in Cochiti! She was also a great cook. She enjoyed cooking all of our traditional foods, which she always prepared from scratch. I

62

remember the many nights she would have Cerelia, Margaret, and me do the grinding of corn or wheat for our daily tortillas, or for the most delicious piki bread. Mother was well known for her expertise in the making of piki bread. The making of piki bread is a long and difficult process, but to mother it was a breeze. She used to experiment with food-colors and milk. She worked at this process until she was satisfied with the results. The processes in making these two types that she used are still in use in Cochiti. Mother loved sharing whatever she had, especially in her recipes, with the ladies of the village. She also helped in teaching ladies to make her piki bread. In fact, she was a very giving person. Most of all, she was a great mother to us, and her death had such a tremendous impact upon us all as a family unit, which is still greatly felt, especially at all of our cultural events.

Mother will always be cherished, and will always be held in the highest regards by all who knew her. I thank God for memories, for she left me so many beautiful ones. Of course, I have my favorites, and those were the times that mother and I went into Santa Fe and made our rounds of the art galleries to deliver her paintings and to take new orders. They were such happy occasions for me. The people were always so happy to see us coming into their shops as they really enjoyed conversing with my mother and me. Mother had such charm and wit that the people enjoyed. I love recalling all of these occasions with my children. In the future, I will do the same for my grandchildren also. I am most proud to be one of her children, and I value very dearly the rich Indian heritage of my mother.

I, the daughter of Tonita Peña, (Quah Ah), married Jose Alcario Melchor on October 12, 1952. We had a traditional wedding in Cochiti. At the request of my father, an old part of the wedding ritual was revived. A ribbon was used, in place of the old common woven sash, to symbolize the knot that God puts on the wedded couple which cannot be untied by anyone but Him. My father remembered the last couple that used it. The original ribbon sash was burned when there was a fire in church in the early eighteen nineties. After the fire,

Tonita at home. Photograph from Joe H. Herrera.

this part of the ritual was abandoned. Currently, a woven Hopi belt or sash has been used for this purpose. The beauty of this symbol has always remained in my memory. Since it was my father who was instrumental in reviving its reuse, it has a very special meaning to me regarding my own marriage.

Cordially yours,

Victoria Maria Melchor

6

Signatures

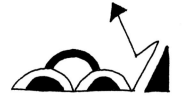

Tonita was very ingenious in the manner in which she signed her paintings. After extensive and careful study of over one hundred of her paintings and signatures, I have come to the conclusion that it is possible to date a number of her paintings, within reason, by the manner in which they were signed.

Joe Herrera told me that when his mother first started painting she signed all of her paintings with her Indian name Quah Ah. I believe this lasted until sometime in 1915. A variation of this signature occurred shortly before or at the time Tonita became pregnant with her second son, Joe H. Herrera, probably in 1917 or 1918. She then modified Quah Ah and used the signature Qua H. AH separating and capitalizing the H in her first name, in honor of her second husband, Herrera. This, I think, was used until the death of Felipe Herrera in 1920. These signatures are rare as Tonita did not paint much at that time.

She began to use her baptismal name,

Tonita Peña   Tonita Peña   Tonita Peña
Cochiti Pueblo

sometimes alone, sometimes with the pueblo name, and sometimes embellished with a decorative motif. She continued using this until she met Epitacio Arquero, in about 1921.

She then used both names in her signatures, one name above the other.

Quah Ah
Tonita Peña

A very few of Tonita's works painted in 1922 and 1923 were signed

Tonita Peña A.   or Tonita P. Arquero

in honor of her husband, Epitacio Arquero. These signatures are also quite rare.

In the early 1930s Tonita began using small combinations of cloud, rain, and storm motifs in conjunction with her name or names, sometimes using the names with the motifs. These became more intricate and complicated in design as time went on, and were used until her death. Remarkably, Tonita never repeated the same design, but always used a different combination on each painting. The headings on each chapter of this book are replicas of these later signature elements.

Signatures and signature elements of the artist used throughout this book were taken from Tonita's work and reproduced by a graphic artist.

66

7

Her Art

In relation to her contemporaries, Tonita's paintings were markedly different. Her style displayed a quiet, friendly and fluid honesty of expression. Like her peers, she never used a ground line or perspective but she managed to give the illusion of depth by avoiding, whenever possible, straight lines of figures. In her dance groups, Tonita's individual figures give the appearance of being alive and moving rather than being fixed in time or motionless as other artists of her time painted.

In her animal dances, Tonita painted groups of dancers to instill an illusion of depth. The singers and chanters have their mouths open wide with song, and their legs and feet are always lifted high with enthusiasm, often wearing necklaces, medicine bags, and sashes. Her deer dancers' toes seem to just touch the ground, giving a feeling of delicacy. When viewing one of her paintings of the Eagle Dance, it seems that the eagles are about to go soaring into space.

Animal Dance, c. 1925. Watercolor. 16 1/2 x 22 inches. Museum of New Mexico Fine Arts Collection.

While Tonita's early paintings of single dance figures tend to be stiff and rigid, her early paintings of ordinary everyday life around the pueblo are peaceful and relate to the viewer feelings of relaxation and serenity.

Tonita would paint a maiden with a water jar on her head and one can see the relaxed, graceful movement as she moved across the plaza of the pueblo. Her scenes of a group of potters polishing, painting, or firing pots are so natural that one can almost hear the women gossip as they work. Some of Tonita's paintings show a woman winnowing wheat in the breeze, with the chaff blowing away from the growing pile of wheat and the woman's skirt gently moving in unison with her arms and the direction of the breeze.

Untitled, undated. Watercolor. 14 x 20 1/2 inches. Penciled on back, "Cochiti Pueblo Indian Plaza Dance, property of L. Petherbridge." Adobe Gallery. Photography by Focus Studio.

Tonita painted what she saw around her without pretense or distortion. One of the delightful features of her paintings is that Tonita never changed her style, although she improved her quality and technique as she continued painting. Even after Tonita moved from San Ildefonso to Cochiti, her style never changed. Tonita expanded her horizons as she developed and experimented over the years. She repeated her subject matter many times during her lifetime. These repetitions were probably most often of the Eagle Dance, the Buffalo Dance, and the Antelope Dance. The repetitions were always different. For instance, paintings of the Eagle Dance might contain one or more dancers. Again, there might be included a drummer or drummers, sometimes with a singer. The clothes would vary with each painting in pattern and in color.

Victory, c. 1943. Watercolor. Museum of New Mexico Fine Arts Collection, negative #31611.

During the war years, while her son, Joe, was in the service, Tonita painted to support the war bond efforts. One of the most unusual paintings executed by Tonita was "Victory," completed in the early days of World War II. When asked why she painted such an unusual piece, Tonita said "It was because of my son, Joe—and the twenty-four other Cochiti boys who are in service."

According to Joe Herrera, Tonita painted the governor and lieutenant governor of the pueblo in the upper left corner by the church. The governor's Lincoln cane of office is decorated with red, white, and blue ribbons and a picture of General McArthur. Opposite the church is the pueblo school with the American flag flying above it.

Missionary Greeting Pueblo Indians, c. 1940. Watercolor. 18 x 20 inches. Made for the Coronado Cuatro Centennial. The Heard Museum #539.

In the foreground, Tonita pictures pueblo life after the war returning to normal. The rich ceremonial life with dancers exiting from the kiva, a pueblo woman baking bread in her horno, an elderly man carrying a bundle of firewood, a field of corn and melons, and animals—both domestic and wild—and a young couple making a ceremonial offering in front of the river bank with its fish.

In the upper center, Tonita painted a large golden V enclosing a red, white, and blue V, for victory, above which is an eagle and an airplane. The seventeen stars, Tonita said, represent the Indian number for victory.

Tonita loved color and used broad stripes in vivid color freely. Her figures are accurate to the last detail and it is said that in painting feathers, she painted each frond separately. James T. Bialac, collector of Indian art and an admirer of Tonita Peña and her work, says that in a group painting of many men or women, upon close examination, each face has some little change of expression or delineation, that no two faces are exactly alike.

A painting in a more traditional style was done during the Coronado Cuatro Centennial, depicting one of Coronado's priests blessing all of the Indian tribal leaders. This painting was done with dignity and in good taste and reflected an Indian's understanding of national and international events.

Tonita was adept at using all of the media at her command. She painted on paper, wood, masonite, and canvas using oils, watercolor, casein, pen, and colored ink. Her large murals, widely exhibited as were her paintings, are still shown in museums all over the United States and in many foreign countries.

Tonita is recognized as a master in her art and is considered by most art experts and collectors to be in a class of her own when compared with other women Indian artists.

Appendix A

Selected Exhibitions

The American Exhibition and Congress, October 21-23, 1937. Tulsa, Oklahoma.

The Annual Indian Market, the Governor's Palace, Santa Fe, New Mexico. Annually in August since 1922. Sponsored by The Southwestern Association of Indian Affairs, Inc.

Third Annual American Indian Week, October 18-22, 1928, Tulsa Fairgrounds. Tulsa, Oklahoma.

Exposition of Indian Tribal Arts, Inc. Sponsored by and circulated through the College Art Association. This major exhibit included 600 examples of art by 21 tribes. First shown in New York City at the Grand Central Galleries for a period of three months beginning in December 1931, it subsequently toured the United States until 1933. Organized by the American painter, John Sloan. Nearly forty museums and private collectors contributed to the exhibit.

The Heard Museum of Anthropology and Primitive Art. Phoenix, Arizona.

Intertribal Indian Ceremonials, held annually five days in August. Gallup, New Mexico.

Museum of New Mexico, Fine Arts Museum, Santa Fe, New Mexico. In most instances, "Contemporary Indian Artists' Annual Exhibition," formerly held during summer.

National Gallery of Art, Washington, D.C. "Contemporary American Indian Painting." October, 1953.

New Mexico State Fair, Albuquerque, New Mexico. Annually, sixteen days in September.

University of Oklahoma European Tours. Sixty paintings assembled by the University College of Fine Arts for the U.S. Information Service in Rome. Shown in nearly a dozen European cities. About half of the exhibit was from the University collections. The remaining works were sent from the H. Adams, Denman, and Dietrich collections, June 1955-May 1956. Forty-seven paintings from the University collection toured Austria and Germany from 1956-1961.

Philbrook Art Center, Tulsa, Oklahoma. In most instances, "Annual American Indian Artists' Exhibition." Held annually since 1946, generally in March.

Appendix B
Selected Collections

American Museum of Natural History,
New York, NY.

New Mexico Museum of Fine Arts,
Santa Fe, NM.

The Amerind Foundation,
Dragoon, AZ.

Gilcrease Institute of American Indian Art,
Tulsa, OK.

School of American Research,
Santa Fe, NM.

The Heard Museum of Anthropology and
Primitive Art, Phoenix, AZ.

Cincinnati Art Museum,
Cincinnati, OH.

Museum of the American Indian, Heye
Foundation, New York, NY.

Cleveland Museum of Art,
Cleveland, OH.

Marion Koogler NcNary Art Institute,
San Antonio, TX.

City Art Museum of St. Louis,
St. Louis, MO.

Katherine Harvey Collection, Museum of
Northern Arizona, Flagstaff, AZ.

Corcoran Gallery of Art,
Washington, DC.

Millicent Rogers Foundation Museum,
Taos, NM.

Cranbrook Institute of Science,
Bloomfield, MI.

The Permanent Collection, New Mexico State
Fair, Albuquerque, NM.

Columbus Gallery of Fine Arts,
Columbus, OH.

University of Oklahoma Library,
Norman, OK.

Robert H. Lowie Museum of Anthropology,
University of California, Berkeley, CA.

University Museum, University of
Pennsylvania, Philadelphia, PA.

Denver Art Museum, Chappell House,
Denver, CO.

Roswell Museum and Art Center,
Roswell, NM.

Dartmouth College Collection, Dartmouth
College, Hanover, MA.

Walter Pierce Museum, East Oregon
College, La Grande, OR.

The Southwest Museum, Los Angeles, CA.

Philbrook Art Center, Tulsa, OK.

References

Alexander, Hartley Burr. *Pueblo Indian Painting.* C. Szwedziki. Nice, France. 1932.

Austin, Mary. *The Land of Journeys Ending.* Century Company, New York. 1924.

Bahti, Tom. *Southwestern Indian Ceremonials.* K.C. Publications, Las Vegas, Nevada. 1968.

Bandelier, Adolph H., and Edgar L. Hewett. *Indians of the Rio Grande Valley.* University of New Mexico Press, Albuquerque. 1937.

Batkin, Jonathan. "Martina Vigil and Florentino Montoya, Master Potters of San Ildefonso and Cochiti Pueblos." *American Indian Art Magazine.* Autumn 1987.

Bloom, Lansing B. "Bourke on the Southwest." XIII, *New Mexico Historical Review.* Vol 13, No 2, pp 192-229. Albuquerque. 1968.

Brody, J.J. *Indian Painters, White Patrons.* University of New Mexico Press, Albuquerque. 1971.

Bywaters, Jerry. *Southwestern Art Today, New Directions, Old Forms In Six Southwestern States.* An exhibition by Dallas Museum of Fine Arts. June 15-September 14, 1947.

Cassidy, Ina Sizer. "Art and Artists of New Mexico." *New Mexico Magazine.* Vol 16, No 11, pp 22, 32-33. Santa Fe. November 1938.

—. "Indian Murals." *New Mexico Magazine,* XII. Santa Fe. 1934.

—. "Tonita Peña (Quah Ah)—Julian Martinez." *New Mexico Magazine,* XI. Santa Fe. November 1933.

Collier, Mrs. Charles S. "Survey of Indian Arts and Crafts." U.S. Bureau of Indian Affairs. Washington, D.C. April 1934.

Dawdy, Doris Ostrander. *Annotated Bibliography of American Indian Painting.* Heye Foundation, New York. 1968.

Dietrich, Margaretta S. "Their Culture Survives." *Indians at Work.* Vol III, No 17, pp 18-24. Office of Indian Affairs, Washington, D.C. April 1936. Also, *New Mexico Magazine,* pp 22, 23, 45. February 1936.

Dorman, Margaret. "A Study of Water Color Paintings of Modern Pueblo Indians." M.A. Thesis, University of New Mexico, Albuquerque.

Dunn, Dorothy. "America's First Painters." *The National Geographic Magazine,* Vol CVII. March 1955.

—. "American Indian Paintings of the Southwest and Plains Areas." *New Mexico Magazine Calendar.* 1934.

—. "Indian Children Carry Forward Old Traditions." *School Arts Magazine,* Vol 34, No 7, pp 426-436. Worcester, Mass. March 1936.

—. *Indian Paintings from the Margaretta S. Dietrich Collection.* The Museum of New Mexico, Santa Fe. 1962.

—. "Opportunities for the Indian Painter." *Smoke Signals.* February 1955.

—. "Pueblo Indian Painting." *Indians at Work.* (Contemporary Arts and Crafts Issue). Undated.

Dutton, Bertha P. "Indians of the Southwest." Southwest Association of Indian Affairs, Santa Fe. 1961.

El Palacio. "At the Gallery." Vol 55, No 10, pp 326-27. Santa Fe. 1948.

—. "At the Gallery." Vol 56, No 6, pp 185. June 1949.

—. "Further Notes on Indian Paintings." Vol 56, No 3. March 1949.

—. "Indian Art Honored." Vol 8, No 7-8, pp 182-183. July 1920.

—. "Indian Artists Visit Museum." Vol 49, No 6. June 1942.

—. "Indians and Indian Life, Exhibit of Indian Paintings." Vol 8, No 5-6, pp 125-127. June 1920.

—. "It is Written." Vol 12, No 7, pp 91-92. April 1962.

—. "New Mexico Painters." Vol 9, No 10, pp 216-18. November 1925.

—. "Painters and Sculptors." Vol 8, No 10-11, pp 237-240. June 1925.

—. "The New Indian Art." Vol 70, No 7-8, pp 39. Spring 1969.

Fergusson, Harvey. *Followers of the Sun*. Alfred A Knopf, New York. 1936.

Fisher, Reginald. *An Art Directory of New Mexico*. Museum of New Mexico School of American Research, Santa Fe. 1947.

Henderson, Alice Corbin. "Indian Artists of the Southwest." *The American Indian*, II. Spring 1945.

Hewett, Edgar Lee. "Native American Artists." *Art and Archaeology*, Vol 13, No 3, pp 103-113. Washington, D.C.

Highwater, Jamake. *Source of the Earth: Early American Indian Painting*. New York Graphic Society, Boston. 1980.

Hogue, Alexander. "Pueblo Tribes Aesthetic Giants, Indian Art Reveals." *El Palacio*. Vol XXIV. March 24, 1928.

"Indian Drawings." *School Arts Magazine*, Vol XXX, pp 461-463. March 1931.

Keleher, William A. *The Fabulous Frontier*. Rydal Press, Santa Fe. 1942.

Kidder, Alfred V. *An Introduction to the Study of Southwestern Archaeology*. Worcester. March 1935.

La Farge, Oliver, and others. "Introduction to American Indian Art; Modern Indian Painting by Alice Corbin Henderson." *Exposition of Indian Tribal Arts*. 1931. Reprinted by Rio Grande Press, 1970.

Lange, Charles H. *Cochiti*. University of Texas Press, Austin. 1959.

Lemos, Pedro J. "Our First American Artists." *School Arts Magazine*, Vol XXXIII. September 1930.

Liggett, Lila Nol. "Artists on the Warpath." *Independent Woman*, Vol XXXIII. February 1944.

Mails, Thomas E. *The Pueblo Children of the Earth Mother*. 2 vols. Doubleday and Company, New York. 1983.

Millington, C. Norris. "American Indian Watercolors." *American Magazine of Art*, Vol XXV. August 1932.

Mitchell, Mary L. "Indian Paintings, The Ideal, The Different Christmas Gift." *New Mexico Magazine*. Vol XXXVIII. December 1960.

New Mexico: A Guide to the Colorful State. Compiled by the Writers' Program of the Works Progress *Administration of New Mexico.* Hastings House, New York. 1940.

"Newark: Paintings by Indians." *Art News.* XXXVL, January 22, 1938.

Pach, Walter. "Notes on the Indian Watercolors." *The Dial.* Vol 68, pp 343-345. New York. 1920.

Pearce, T.M. *New Mexico Place Names.* University of New Mexico Press, Albuquerque. 1965.

Peterson, Susan. *The Living Tradition of Maria Martinez.* Kodansha, New York. 1977.

"Pueblo Children Represent United States in an International Art Exhibit." *Indians At Work,* II, Feb. 15, 1935.

"Pueblo Indian Painting." New Mexico Association of Indian Affairs, *Indian Art Series,* No 1.

Rush, Olive. "Young Indians at Work in Old Forms." *Theatre Arts Monthly,* Vol XVII. August 1933.

"Scalped." *Art Digest,* XV, October 1, 1940.

Snodgrass, Jeanne O. *American Indian Painters, A Biographical Directory.* Museum of the American Indian Heye Foundation, New York. 1968.

Spivey, Richard L. *Maria.* Northland Press, Flagstaff. 1979.

Spinder, Herbert J. *Artists of the Southwest.* Vol XCV. International Studio. February 1930.

—. "Fine Arts and the First Americans." *Indians at Work,* Vol III. January 15, 1936. Also, *Introduction to American Indian Art, Part II,* New York. The Exposition of Indian Tribal Arts, Inc. 1931.

Stanley, F. *The San Ildefonso Story.* Nazareth, TX. Edition of 400 copies.

Tanner, Clara Lee. "Contemporary Indian Art." *Arizona Highways.* Vol 26, No 2, pp 12-29. Phoenix. 1950.

—. *Southwest Indian Paintings: A Changing Art.* 2nd Edition. University of Arizona Press,

—. *The James T. Bialac Collection of Southwest Indian Paintings*. Arizona State Museum, University of Arizona, Tucson. 1968.

Twitchell, Ralph Emerson. *The Leading Facts of New Mexico History*. Torch Press, Cedar Rapids, Iowa. 1911.

"Two Paintings of Tonita Peña and an Article on Her Work." *Christian Science Monitor*. Weekly Magazine Section. April 22, 1936.

Underhill, Ruth. *Pueblo Crafts*. Bureau of Indian Affairs, Washington, D.C. 1944.

Waters, Frank. *Masked Gods*. University of New Mexico Press, Albuquerque. 1950.

Other Titles Available

C.N. Cotton and His Navajo Blankets *by Lester L. Williams, M.D.*
A biography of the premier Navajo trader and blanket dealer accompanied by reprints of his mail order catalogs dating from 1896. 102 pages, 13 color plates, 48 black and white plates, softbound, $22.50.

The Mimbres, Art and Archaeology *by Jesse Walter Fewkes. Introduction by J. J. Brody*
Three essays, originally published between 1914 and 1934, on these aborigines from southern New Mexico. 182 pages, 300 illustrations, hardbound $29.95, softbound $16.95.

A Little History of the Navajos *by Oscar H. Lipps*
A reprint of a 1909 concise and authentic history of the Navajo Indians. 136 pages, 16 black and white photographs, hardbound, $19.95.

Zuni Fetishism *by Ruth Kirk*
Originally published in 1948 by El Palacio, Journal of Museum of New Mexico, this study of twenty-five different pieces collected by the Laboratory of Anthropology brings an expanded understanding to the examination of this aspect of Zuni religion and ceremonialism. 72 pages, 10 black and white photographs, softbound, $4.75.

J.B. Moore, United States Licensed Indian Trader: A Collection of Catalogs Published at Crystal Trading Post, 1903-1911 *Introduction by Marian Rodee*
Catalogs of fine Navajo rugs, ceremonial baskets, silverware, jewelry, and curios originally published by Moore. 114 pages, 30 color plates, black and white photographs, softbound, $16.50.

Pendleton Woolen Mills *Introduction by E.W. Haggerty*
A reprint of the 1915 mail order catalog from the world famous Pendleton Woolen Mills of Oregon, featuring photographs of patterns, Indians, daily uses and a history of the Mills. 40 pages, full color, softbound, $8.50.

The Navajo *by J.B. Moore*
An early mail order catalog, first printed in 1911. 40 pages, 15 color plates, 17 black and white photographs, softbound, $12.50.

Hopi Snake Ceremonies *by Jesse Walter Fewkes*
A reprint of two essays dating from 1894 and 1897, describing and picturing in detail one of the most famous and spectacular of all Native American ceremonial events. These ceremonies are now closed to non-Indians. 160 pages, 51 black and white plates, softbound, $16.95.

Shipping costs will be additional

Avanyu Publishing Inc.
P.O. Box 27134, Albuquerque, N.M. 87125
(505)243-8485   (505)266-6128